BEETHOVEN

SUPER EASY SONGBOOK

ISBN 978-1-5400-9191-8

Visit Hal Leonard Online at
www.halleonard.com

Contact us:
Hal Leonard
7777 West Bluemound Road
Milwaukee, WI 53213
Email: info@halleonard.com

In Europe, contact:
Hal Leonard Europe Limited
42 Wigmore Street
Marylebone, London, W1U 2RN
Email: info@halleonardeurope.com

In Australia, contact:
Hal Leonard Australia Pty. Ltd.
4 Lentara Court
Cheltenham, Victoria, 3192 Australia
Email: info@halleonard.com.au

Welcome to the *Super Easy Songbook* series!

This unique collection will help you play your favorite songs quickly and easily. Here's how it works:

- Play the simplified melody with your right hand. Letter names appear inside each note to assist you.

- There are no key signatures to worry about! If a sharp ♯ or flat ♭ is needed, it is shown beside the note each time.

- There are no page turns, so your hands never have to leave the keyboard.

- If two notes are connected by a tie ⌣, hold the first note for the combined number of beats. (The second note does not show a letter name since it is not re-struck.)

- Add basic chords with your left hand using the provided keyboard diagrams. Chord voicings have been carefully chosen to minimize hand movement.

- The left-hand rhythm is up to you, and chord notes can be played together or separately. Be creative!

- If the chords sound muddy, move your left hand an octave* higher. If this gets in the way of playing the melody, move your right hand an octave higher as well.

  * *An octave spans eight notes. If your starting note is C, the next C to the right is an octave higher.*

――――――――――――――― ALSO AVAILABLE ―――――――――――――――

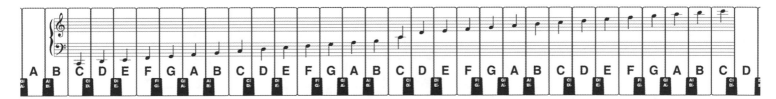

Hal Leonard Student Keyboard Guide HL00296039

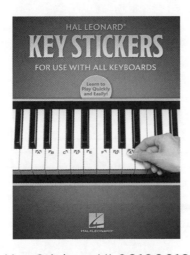

Key Stickers HL00100016

Choral Fantasy

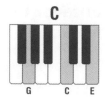
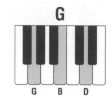
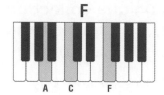

By Ludwig van Beethoven

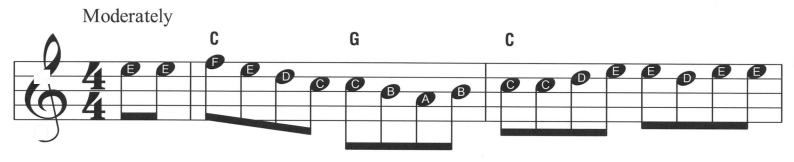

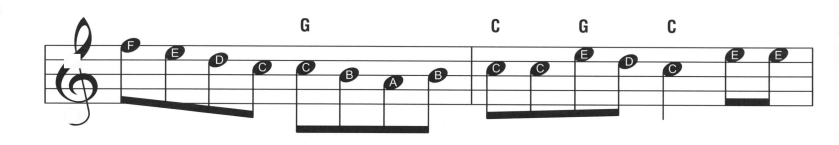

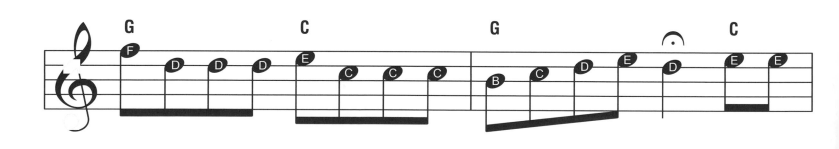

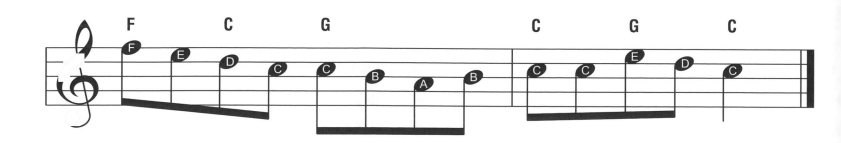

Ecossaise No. 1

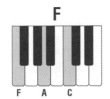
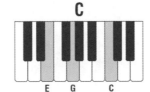
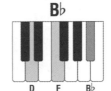
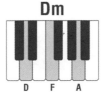

By Ludwig van Beethoven

Für Elise

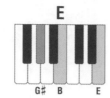

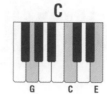
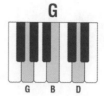

Moderately, with motion
(no chord)

By Ludwig van Beethoven

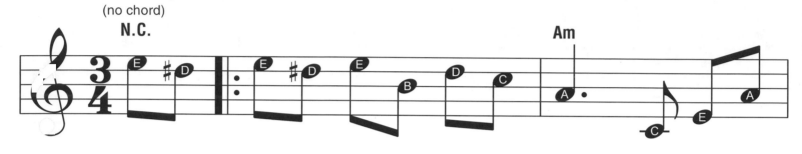

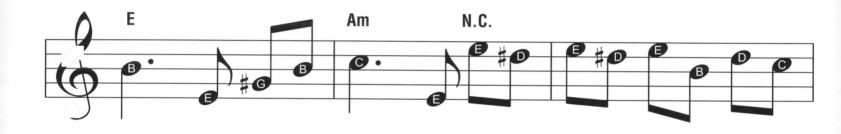

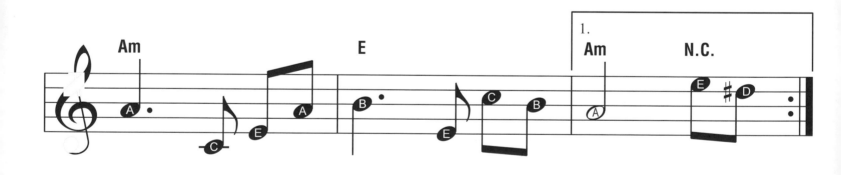

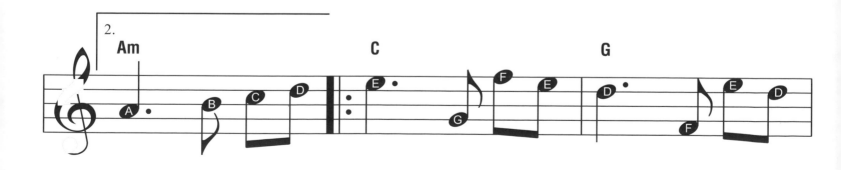

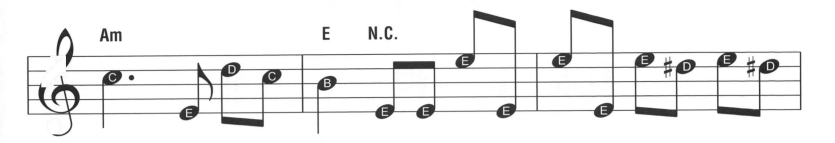

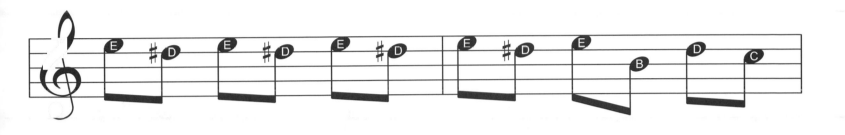

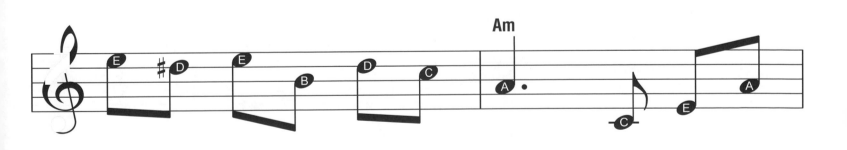

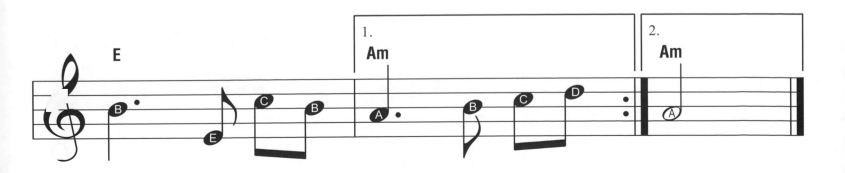

Menuett

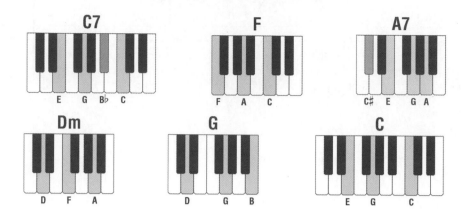

By Ludwig van Beethoven

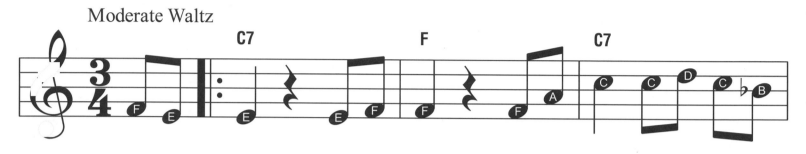

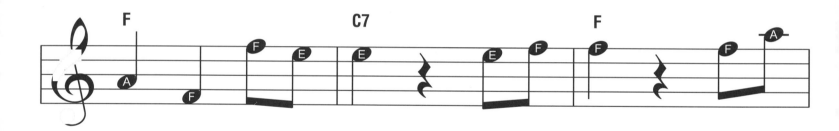

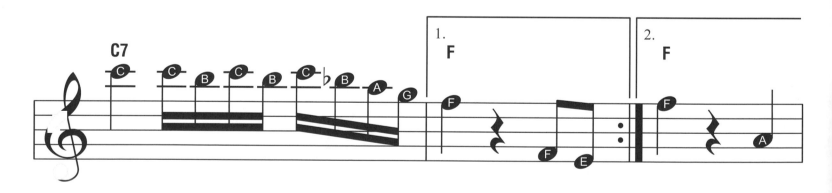

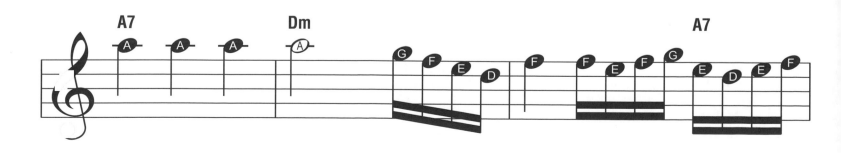

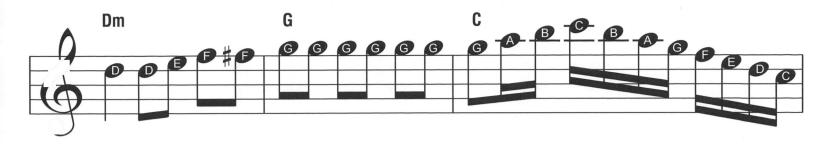

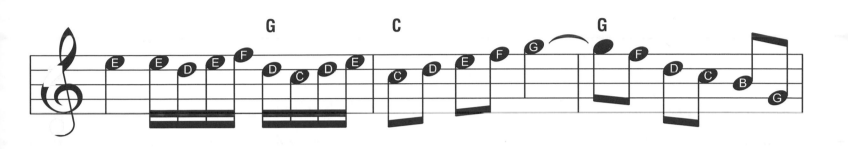

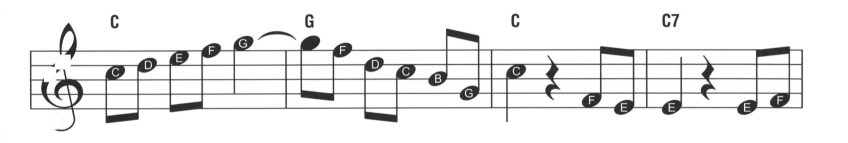

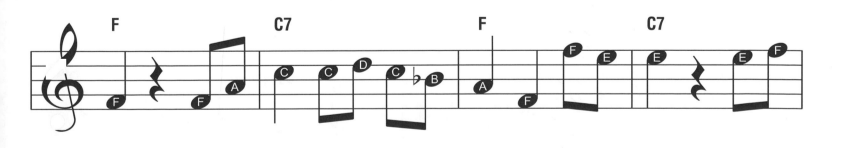

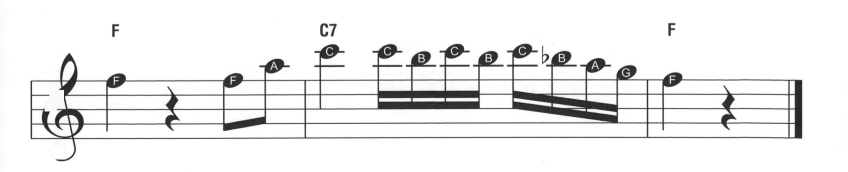

Minuet in G Major

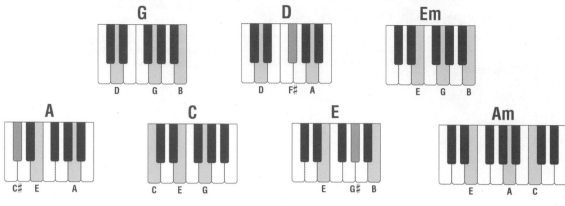

By Ludwig van Beethoven

Piano Concerto No. 5
("Emperor")
First Movement

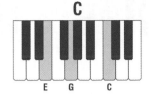
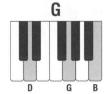

By Ludwig van Beethoven

Piano Concerto No. 3
Third Movement

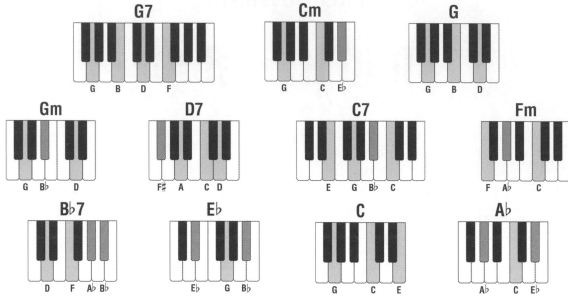

By Ludwig van Beethoven

Piano Sonata No. 8
("Pathetique")
Second Movement

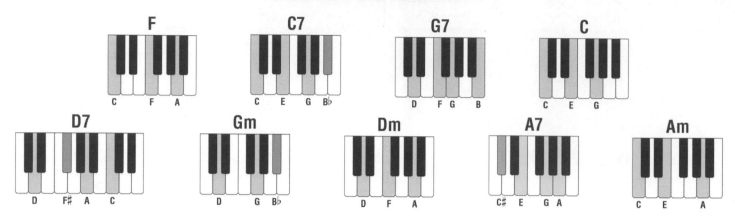

By Ludwig van Beethoven

Moderately slow

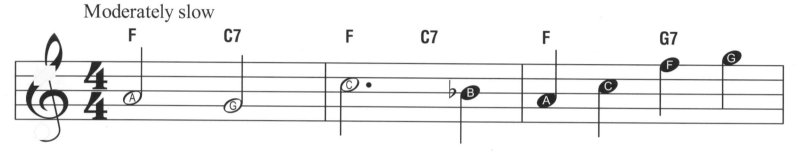

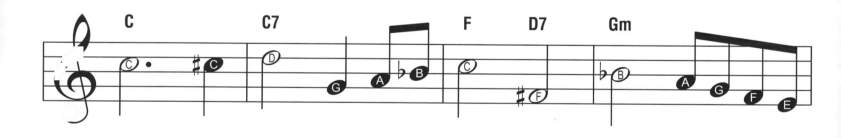

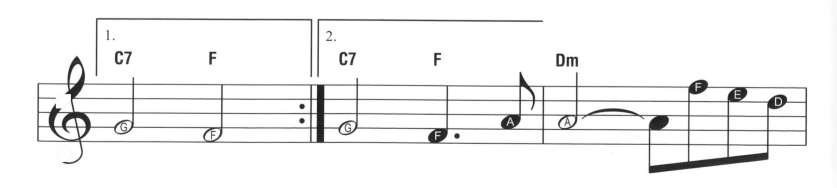

Piano Sonata No. 14
("Moonlight")
First Movement

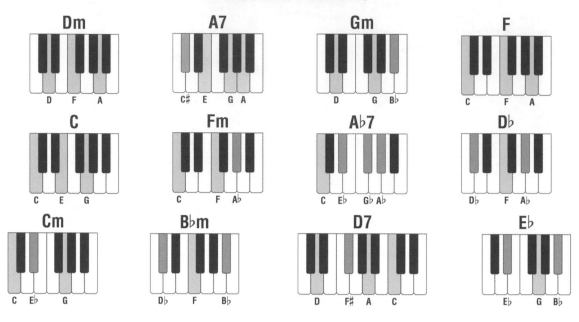

By Ludwig van Beethoven

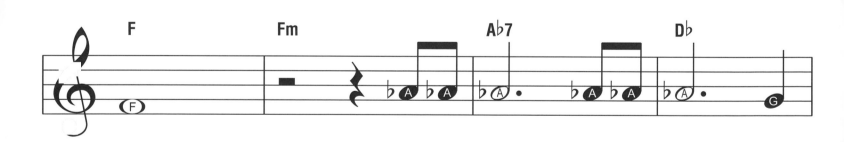

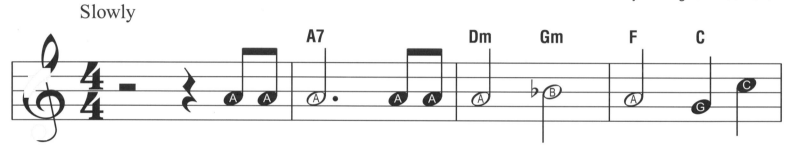

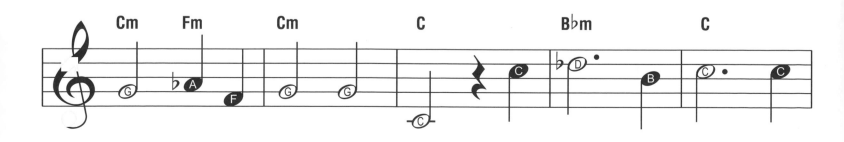

Piano Sonata No. 15
("Pastoral")
Second Movement

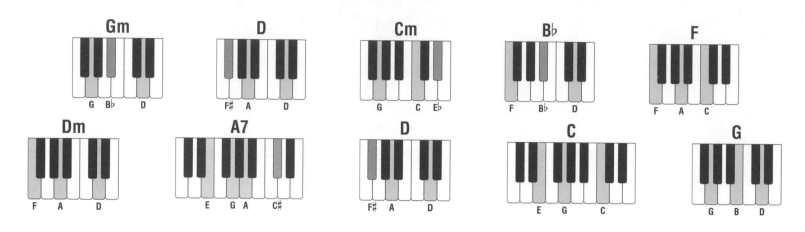

By Ludwig van Beethoven

Moderately slow

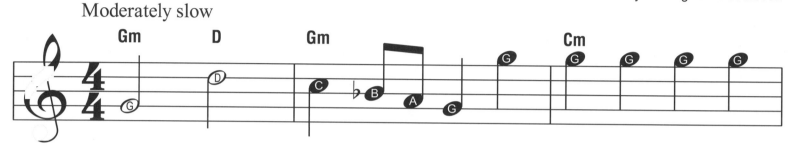

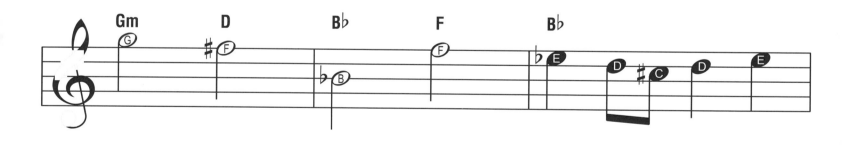

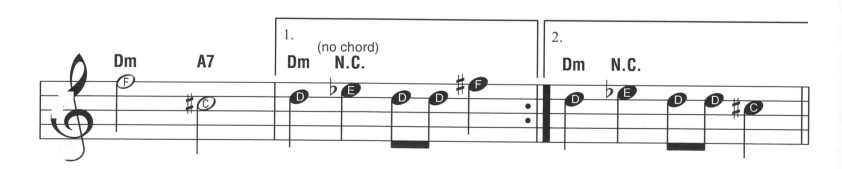

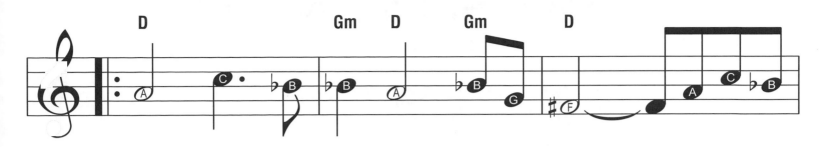

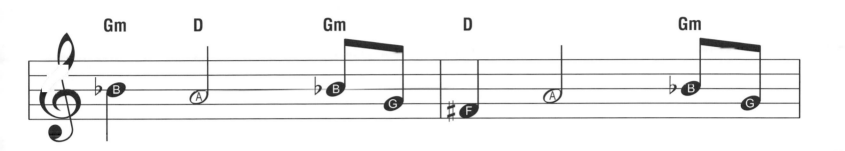

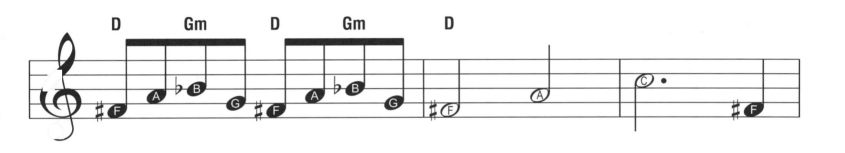

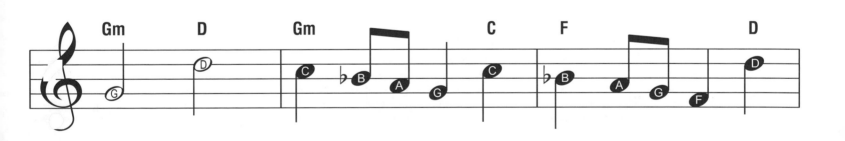

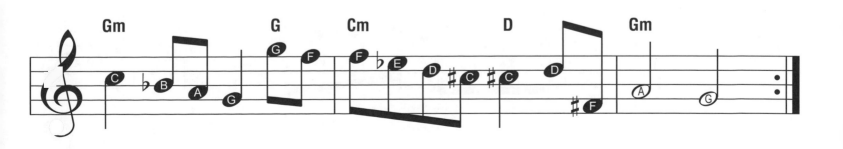

Piano Sonata No. 19
First Movement

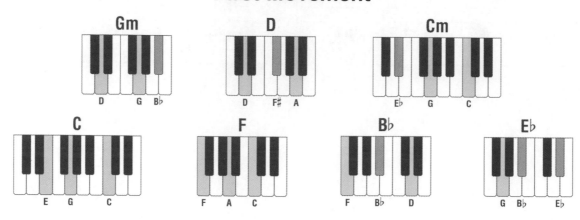

By Ludwig van Beethoven

Moderately

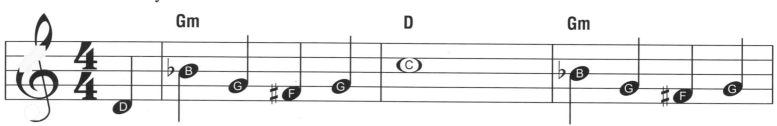

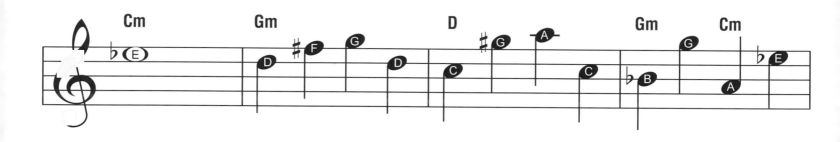

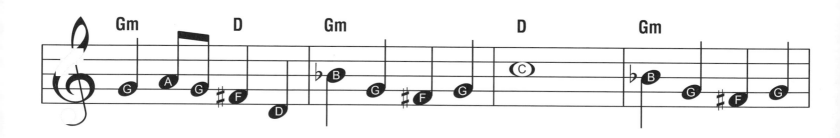

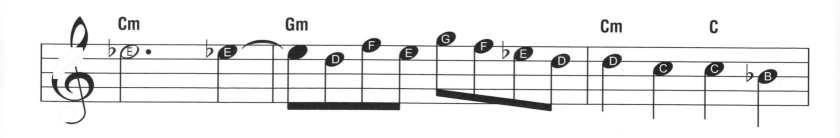

Russian Folk Song

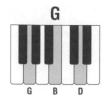
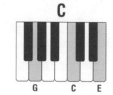
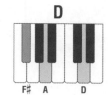

By Ludwig van Beethoven

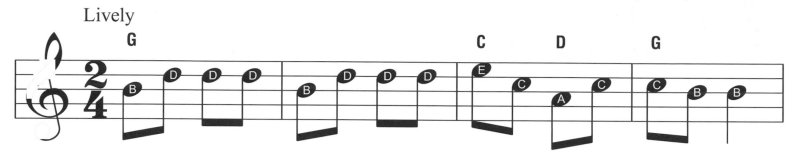

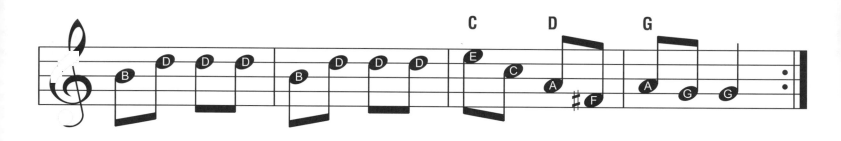

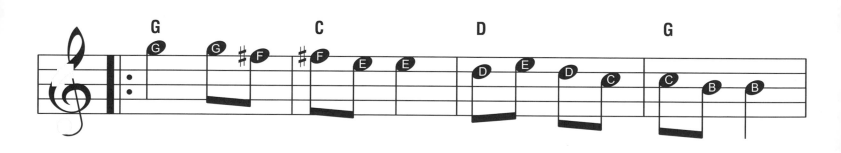

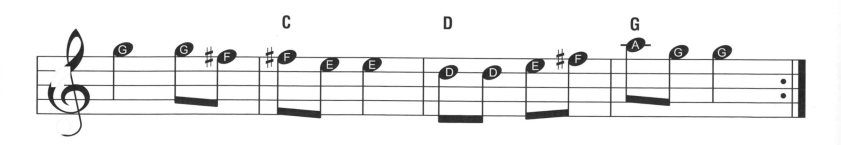

Symphony No. 6
("Pastoral")
Fifth Movement

By Ludwig van Beethoven

Sonatina in G Major
First Movement

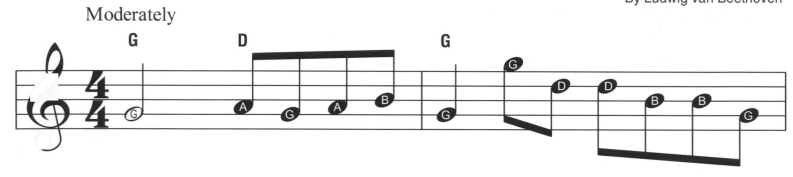

By Ludwig van Beethoven

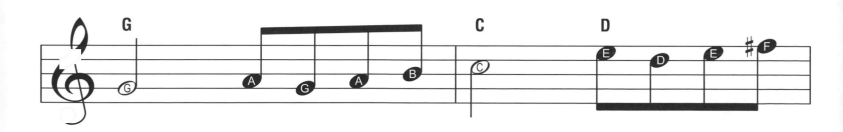

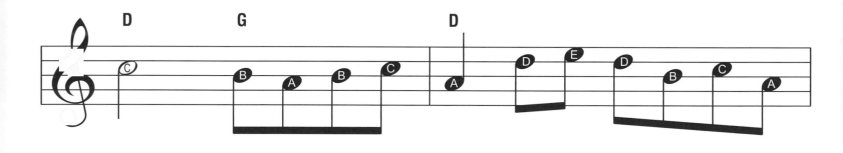

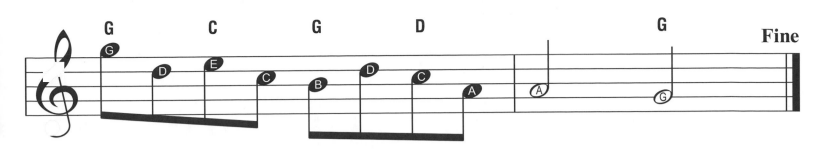

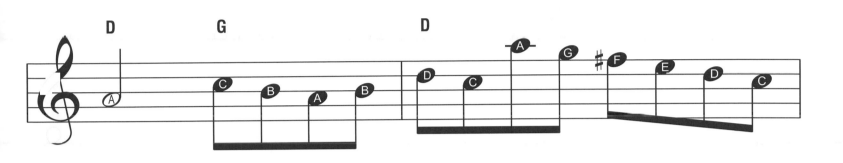

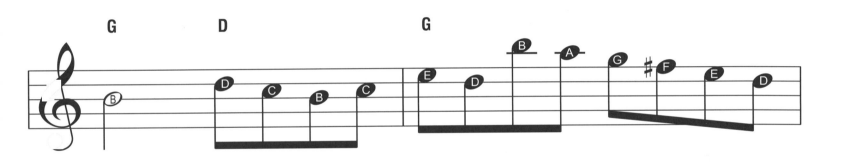

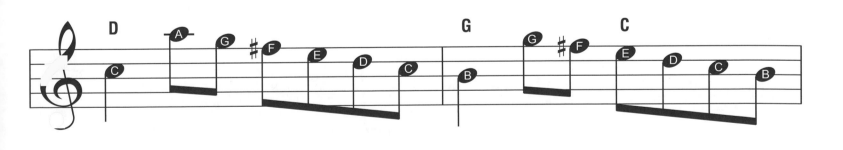

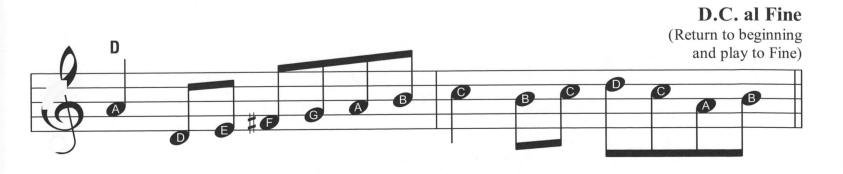

Symphony No. 3
("Eroica")
First Movement

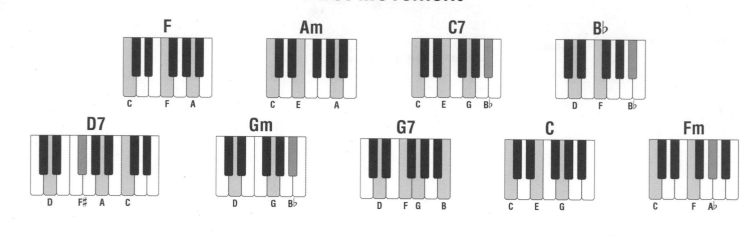

By Ludwig van Beethoven

Majestically

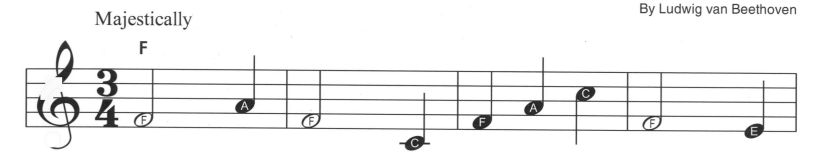

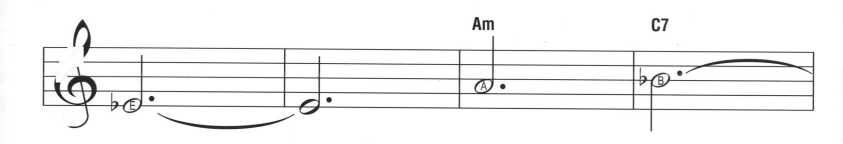

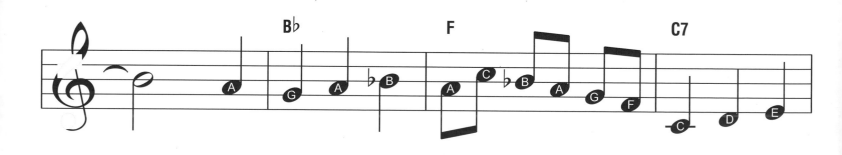

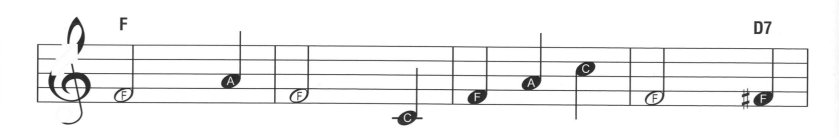

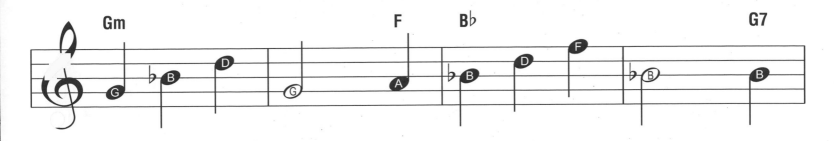

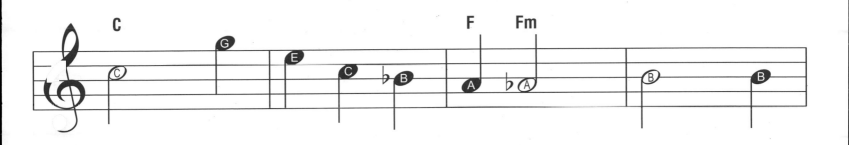

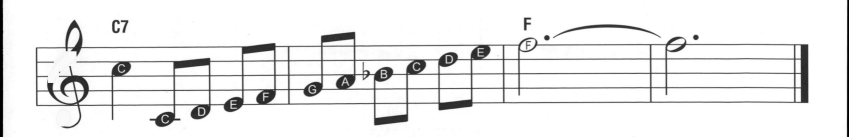

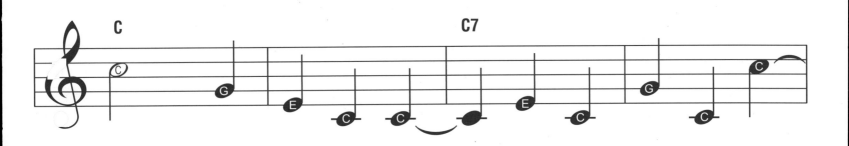

Symphony No. 5
First Movement

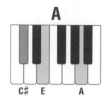
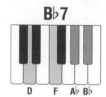
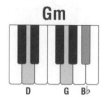
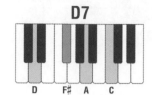

By Ludwig van Beethoven

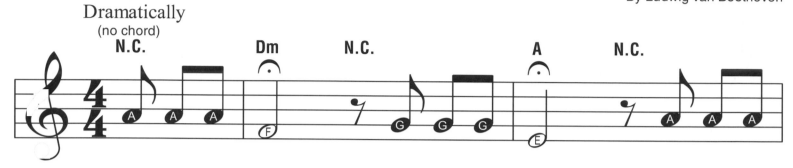

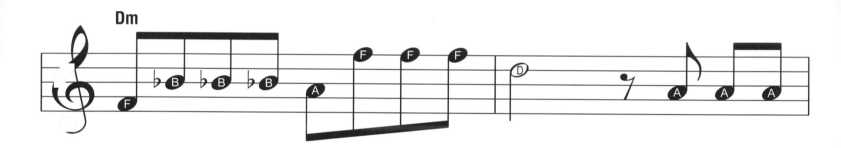

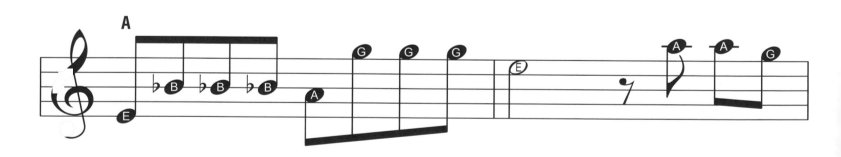

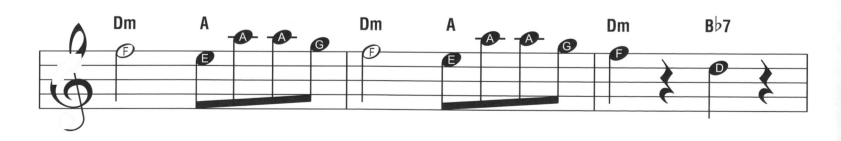

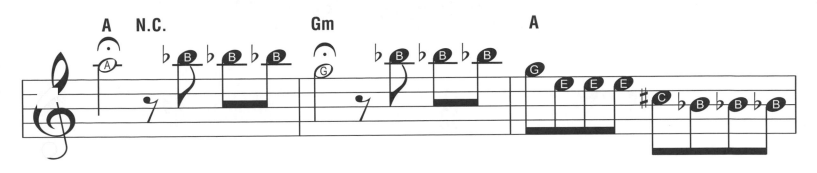

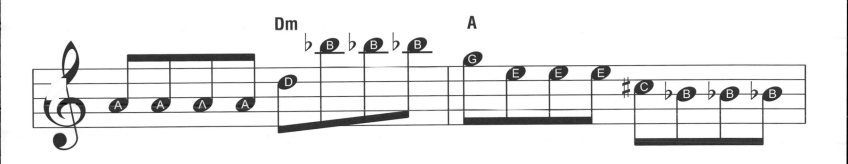

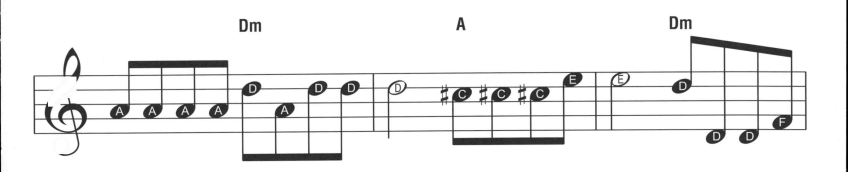

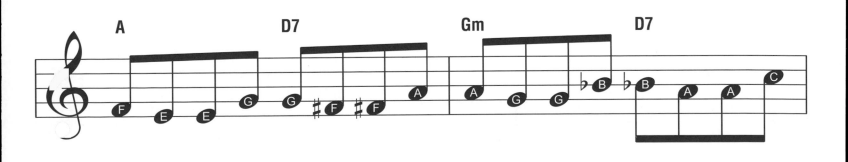

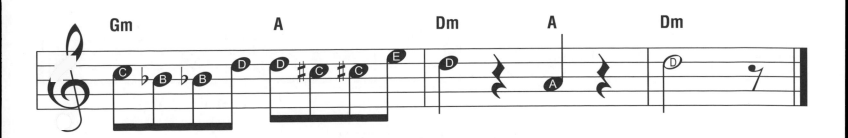

Symphony No. 7
Second Movement

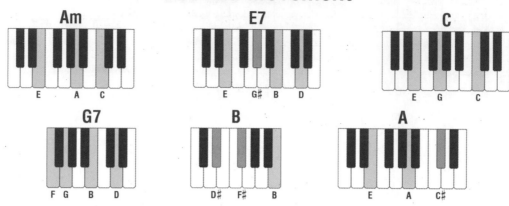

By Ludwig van Beethoven

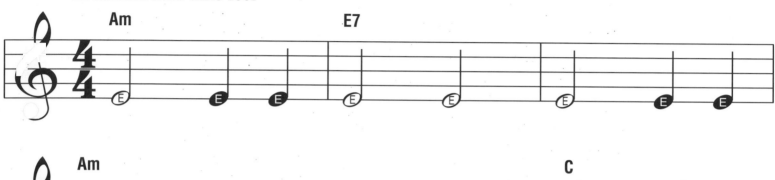

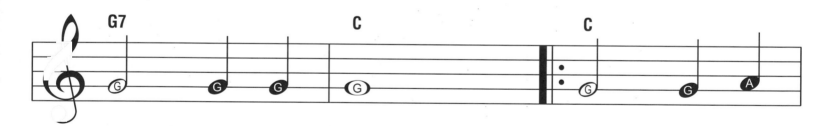

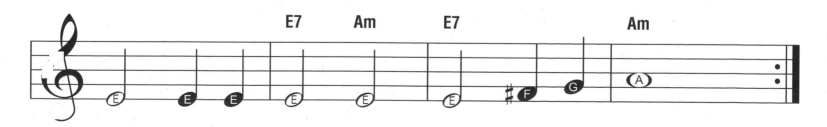

Symphony No. 9
Fourth Movement ("Ode to Joy")

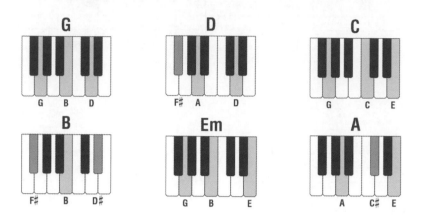

By Ludwig van Beethoven

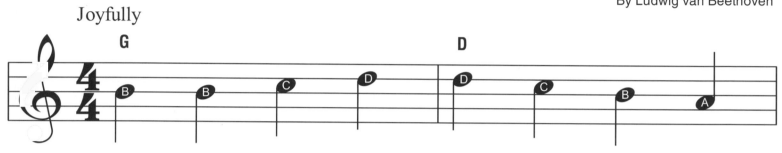

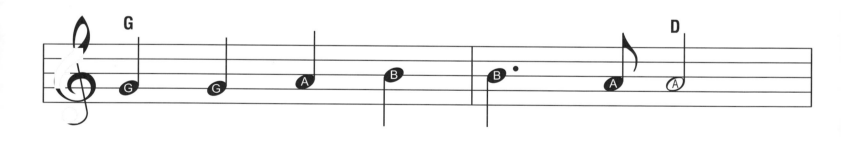

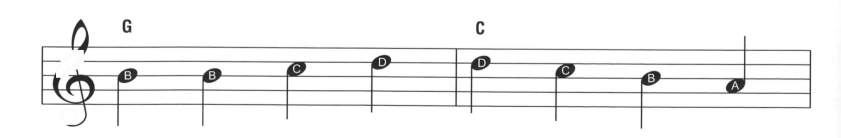

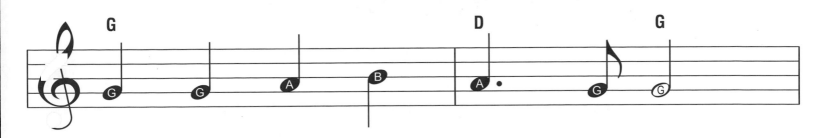

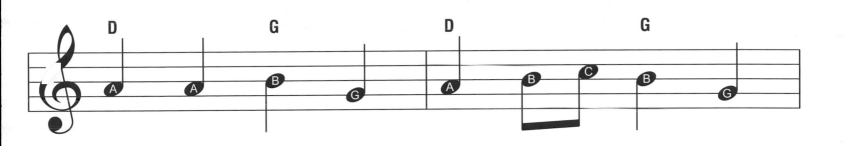

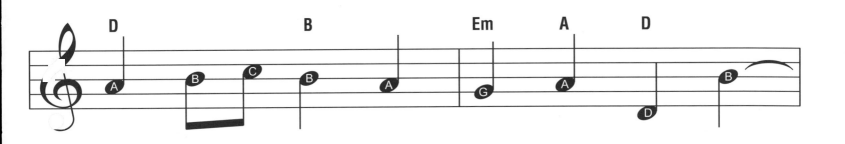

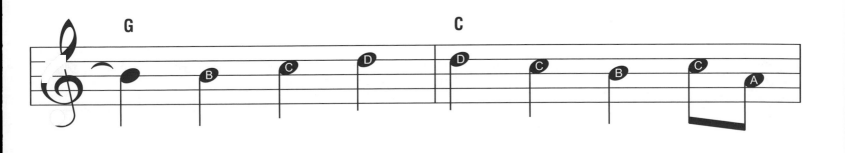

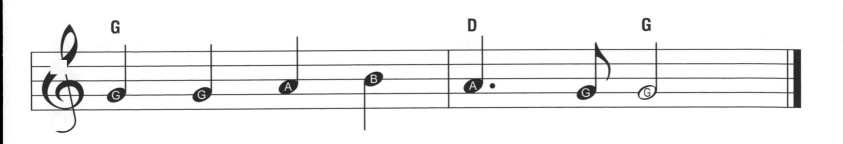

Turkish March
from THE RUINS OF ATHENS

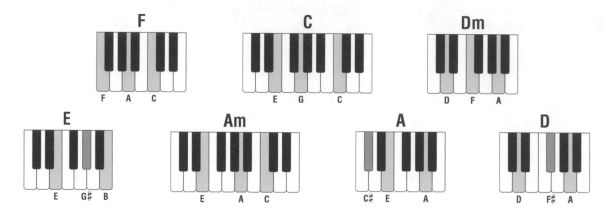

By Ludwig van Beethoven

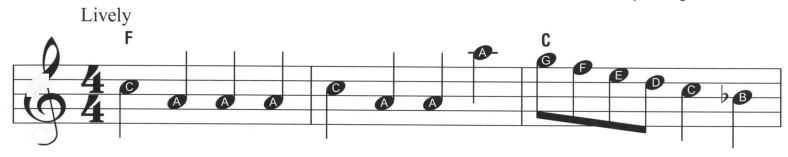

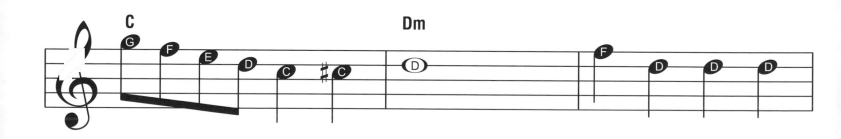

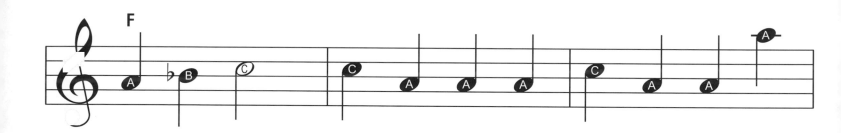

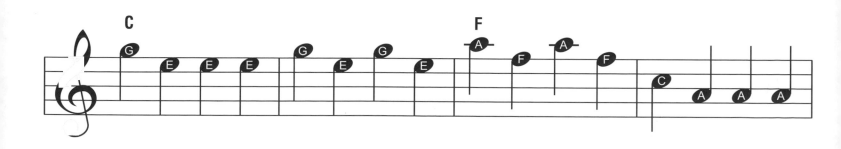

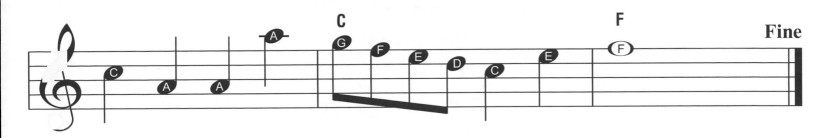
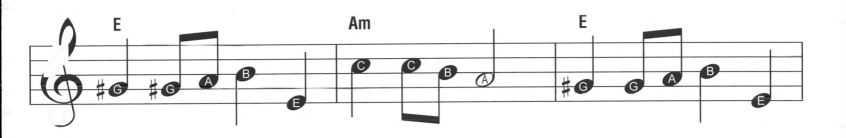
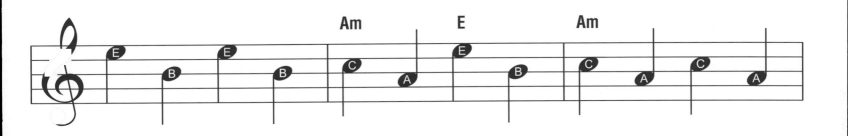
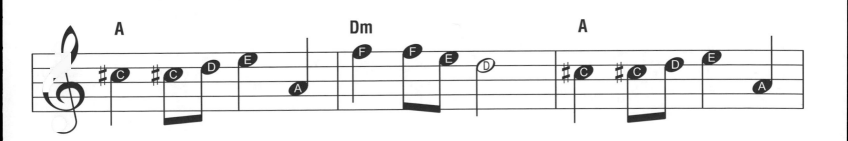
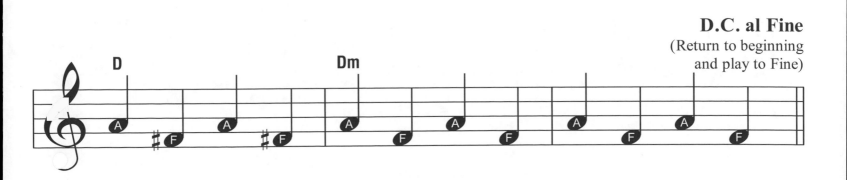

Violin Concerto
Third Movement

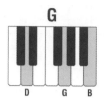
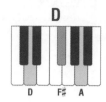
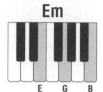
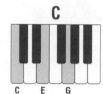

By Ludwig van Beethoven

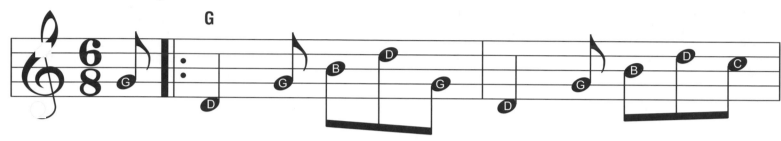

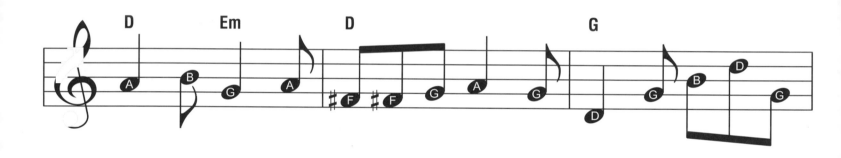

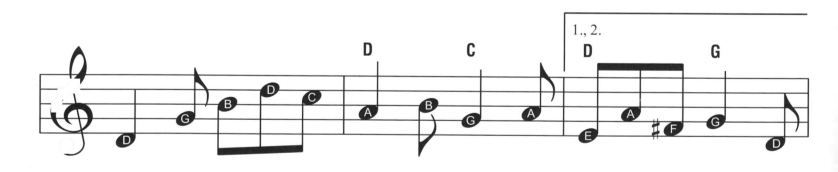

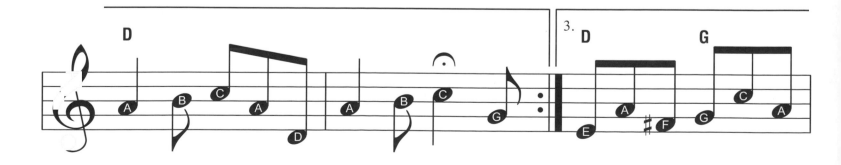

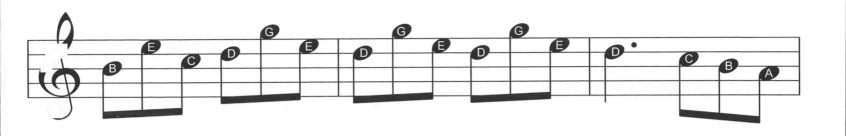

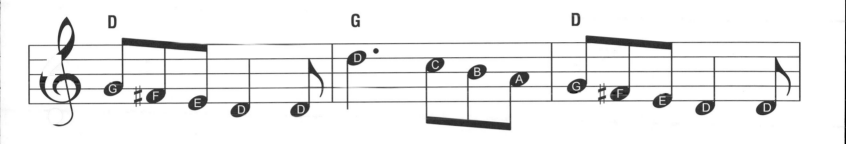

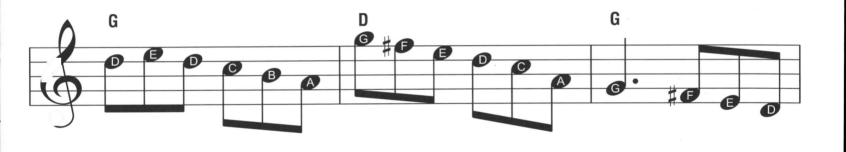

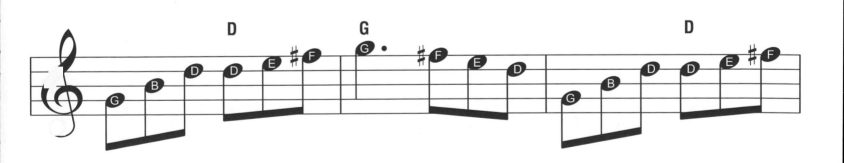

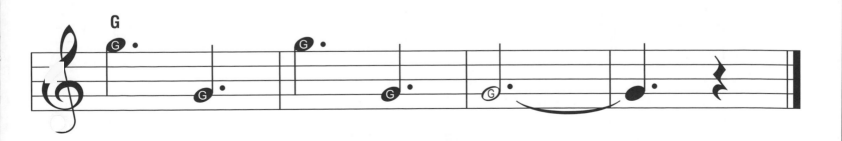

Wellington's Victory

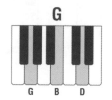
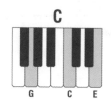
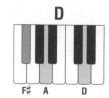
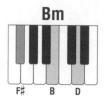
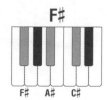

Bright Waltz

By Ludwig van Beethoven

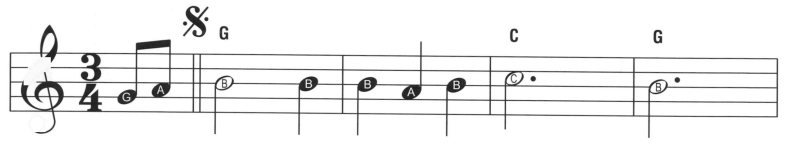

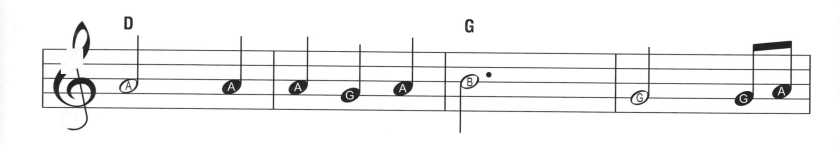

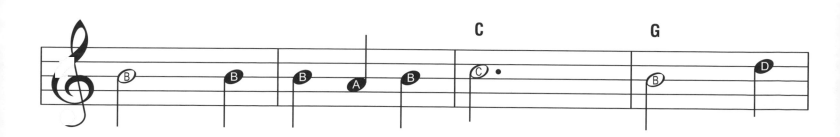

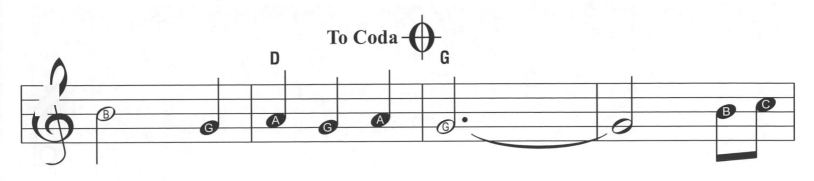

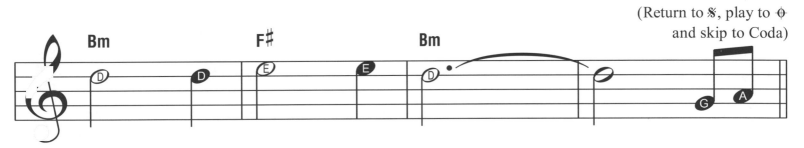

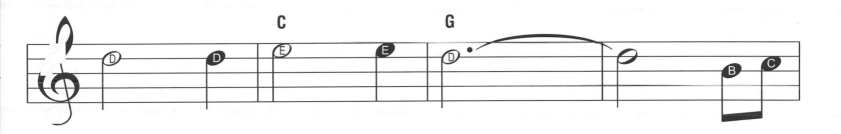

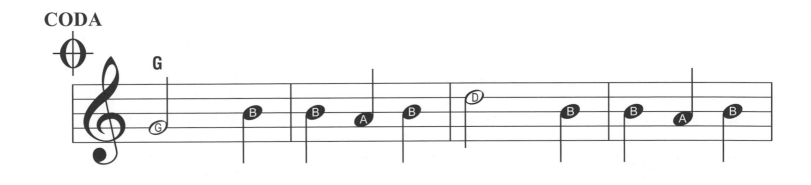

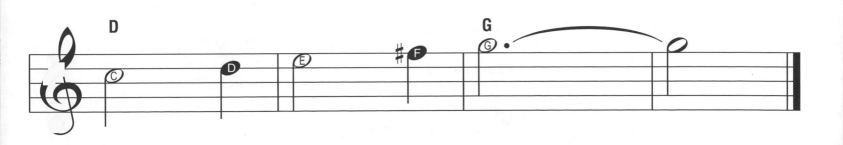

SUPER EASY SONGBOOK

It's super easy! This series features accessible arrangements for piano, with simple right-hand melody, letter names inside each note, and basic left-hand chord diagrams. Perfect for players of all ages!

THE BEATLES
00198161 60 songs $15.99

BEAUTIFUL BALLADS
00385162 50 songs $14.99

BEETHOVEN
00345533 21 selections $9.99

BEST SONGS EVER
00329877 60 songs $15.99

BROADWAY
00193871 60 songs $15.99

JOHNNY CASH
00287524 20 songs $9.99

CHART HITS
00380277 24 songs $12.99

CHRISTMAS CAROLS
00277955 60 songs $15.99

CHRISTMAS SONGS
00236850 60 songs $15.99

CHRISTMAS SONGS WITH 3 CHORDS
00367423 30 songs $10.99

CLASSIC ROCK
00287526 60 songs $15.99

CLASSICAL
00194693 60 selections $15.99

COUNTRY
00285257 60 songs $15.99

DISNEY
00199558 60 songs $15.99

BOB DYLAN
00364487 22 songs $12.99

BILLIE EILISH
00346515 22 songs $10.99

FOLKSONGS
00381031 60 songs $15.99

FOUR CHORD SONGS
00249533 60 songs $15.99

FROZEN COLLECTION
00334069 14 songs $10.99

GEORGE GERSHWIN
00345536 22 songs $9.99

GOSPEL
00285256 60 songs $15.99

HIT SONGS
00194367 60 songs $15.99

HYMNS
00194659 60 songs $15.99

JAZZ STANDARDS
00233687 60 songs $15.99

BILLY JOEL
00329996 22 songs $10.99

ELTON JOHN
00298762 22 songs $10.99

KIDS' SONGS
00198009 60 songs $15.99

LEAN ON ME
00350593 22 songs $9.99

THE LION KING
00303511 9 songs $9.99

ANDREW LLOYD WEBBER
00249580 48 songs $19.99

MOVIE SONGS
00233670 60 songs $15.99

PEACEFUL MELODIES
00367880 60 songs $16.99

POP SONGS FOR KIDS
00346809 60 songs $16.99

POP STANDARDS
00233770 60 songs $15.99

QUEEN
00294889 20 songs $10.99

ED SHEERAN
00287525 20 songs $9.99

SIMPLE SONGS
00329906 60 songs $15.99

STAR WARS (EPISODES I-IX)
00345560 17 songs $10.99

TAYLOR SWIFT
00323195 22 songs $10.99

THREE CHORD SONGS
00249664 60 songs $15.99

TOP HITS
00300405 22 songs $10.99

WORSHIP
00294871 60 songs $15.99

www.halleonard.com